I CAN MAKE IT!

papier-mâché

Susan Moxley

Series by Diane James & Sara Lynn

2 Techniques

4 Paper Plates

6 Picture Frames

8 Napkin Rings

10 Badges

12 Bangles and Beads

14 Bowls

16 Animals

20 Masks

24 Index

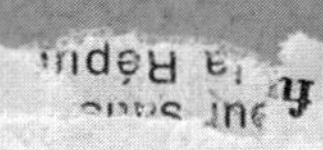

TWO-CAN

Techniques

In this book, we will be looking at a craft called 'papier-mâché'.
The words mean 'chewed paper' in French. Papier-mâché is made by building up layers of newspaper and paste over a mould. The paste makes the paper soggy so that it is easy to work with. When the paper dries, it becomes hard and fairly strong.

Paste

We made our paste from flour, salt and water. Put half a cup of flour and a large spoon of salt into a bowl. Add about half a cup of water, a little at a time, and stir the mixture well. When it is thick and creamy, the paste is ready to use.

Paper Strips

Tear strips of newspaper using a ruler to help you. Use short strips of paper for working on small shapes, and longer strips for big objects. Spread paste on to the paper strips with your fingers, or a paste brush. You will need to paste on three or four layers of paper strips to make papier-mâché objects.

newspaper strips

paste

Papier-Mâché

All sorts of things make good moulds for using with papier-mâché. One of the best is a blown-up balloon. Cover it with three or four layers of paste and newspaper strips. Leave the paste to dry – it might take a day or more. When the paste is dry, you can burst the balloon, leaving your papier-mâché in one piece. Or, you can gently ease the papier-mâché off the balloon.

balloon

plastic container

Empty plastic containers also make good moulds. It is not necessary to take the containers out when you have finished pasting on your newspaper strips. You can also cut out shapes from cardboard and paste newspaper strips over them.

cardboard shape

Paper Plates

Making a colourful plate is a good papier-mâché project to start with.

Ready, steady, go…

1 Use three paper plates piled on top of each other. This will make your finished plate stronger.

2 Tear some newspaper into strips and make up some paste.

3 Cover the plates all over with several layers of paste and paper.

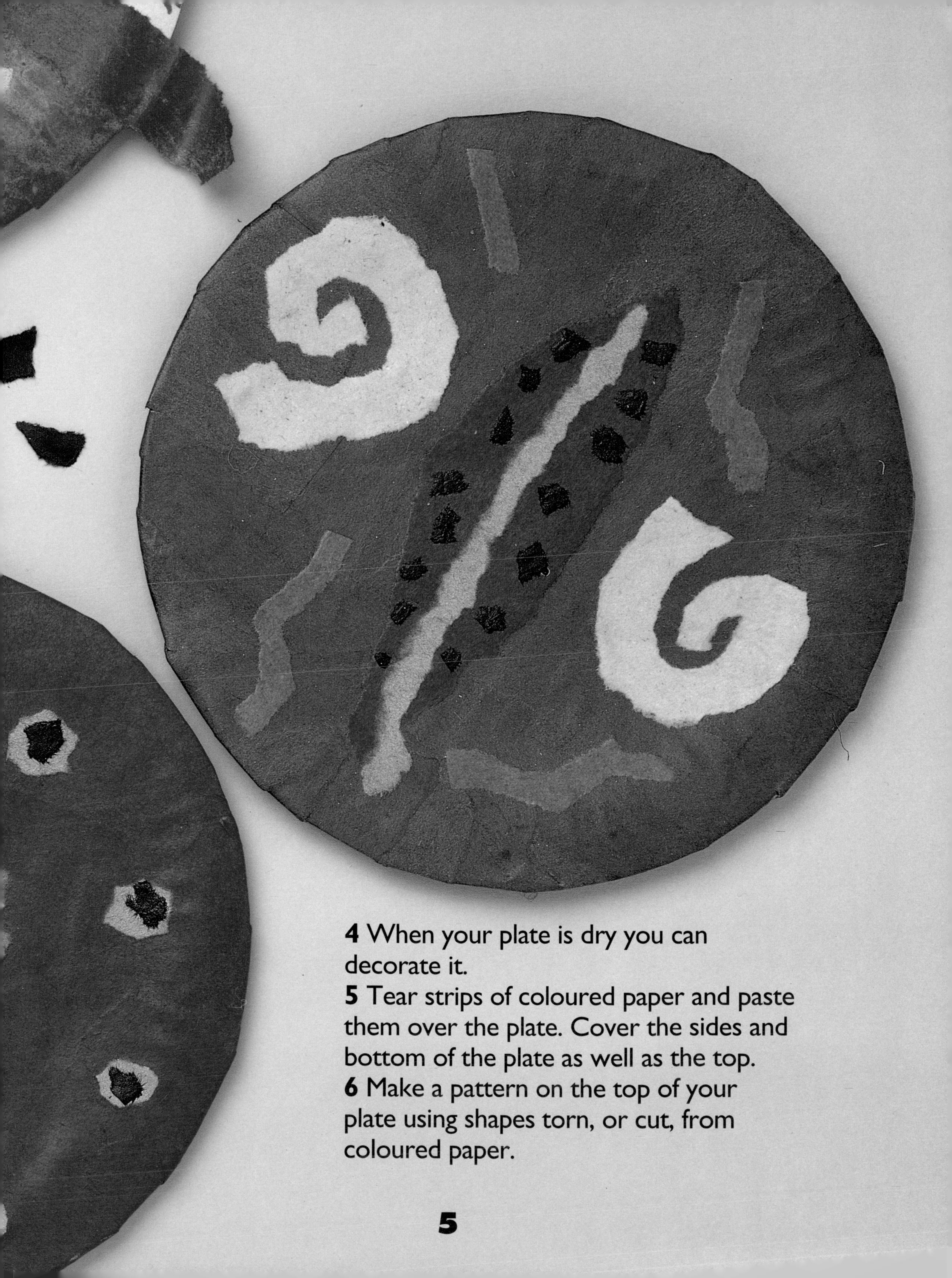

4 When your plate is dry you can decorate it.
5 Tear strips of coloured paper and paste them over the plate. Cover the sides and bottom of the plate as well as the top.
6 Make a pattern on the top of your plate using shapes torn, or cut, from coloured paper.

Picture Frames

Here is a way to make a picture frame for your favourite photo or painting.

Ready, steady, go…

1 You will need a piece of thick cardboard, slightly larger than the picture you want to frame.

2 Ask a grown-up to cut a rectangle from the middle of the cardboard. This should be slightly smaller than your picture.

3 Cover the frame with several layers of paste and newspaper strips.

4 When the frame is dry you can paint it in bright colours.

Or, you could tear shapes out of coloured paper and paste them on as you did for paper plates.

5 Next, tape your painting or photograph to the back of the frame.

Napkin Rings

These brightly coloured napkin holders are very useful and they look good on the table, too! You could make a set for a special present.

Ready, steady, go…

1 Cut a length off a cardboard tube, about four centimetres wide.

2 Decide what shape you want to put on your holder. We made a bird, a tiger and a crown.

3 Draw your shape on a piece of thin cardboard and cut it out.
4 Tape the shape on to your small tube.
5 Tear some newspaper into small strips and make some paste.
6 Cover the tube and cardboard shape with layers of paper strips and paste.
7 Once your napkin ring is dry, you can decorate it. Why not try splattering some paint on!

Badges

Just one of these colourful badges will brighten up your dungarees or T-shirt. You could make a collection and give some to your friends!

Ready, steady, go…

1 Decide on a shape for your badge and cut it out of cardboard.

2 Cover the shape with several layers of newspaper strips and paste. Leave it to dry.

3 Ask a grown-up to fasten a safety pin on to the back of the badge with a couple of strips of paper and paste.

4 Paint your badge in bright colours. You could paint your name on it!

Ask a grown-up to help you pin your badge on.

Bangles and Beads

Make some bangles and beads to cheer up a plain outfit, or to give away as presents.

Bangles

1 Cut a strip of thin cardboard that will fit around your wrist. It should slip on and off easily. Tape the ends together.

2 Cover your cardboard bangle with layers of newspaper strips and paste. Leave it to dry.

3 Paint the bangle using bright colours. When it is dry, it will be ready to wear.

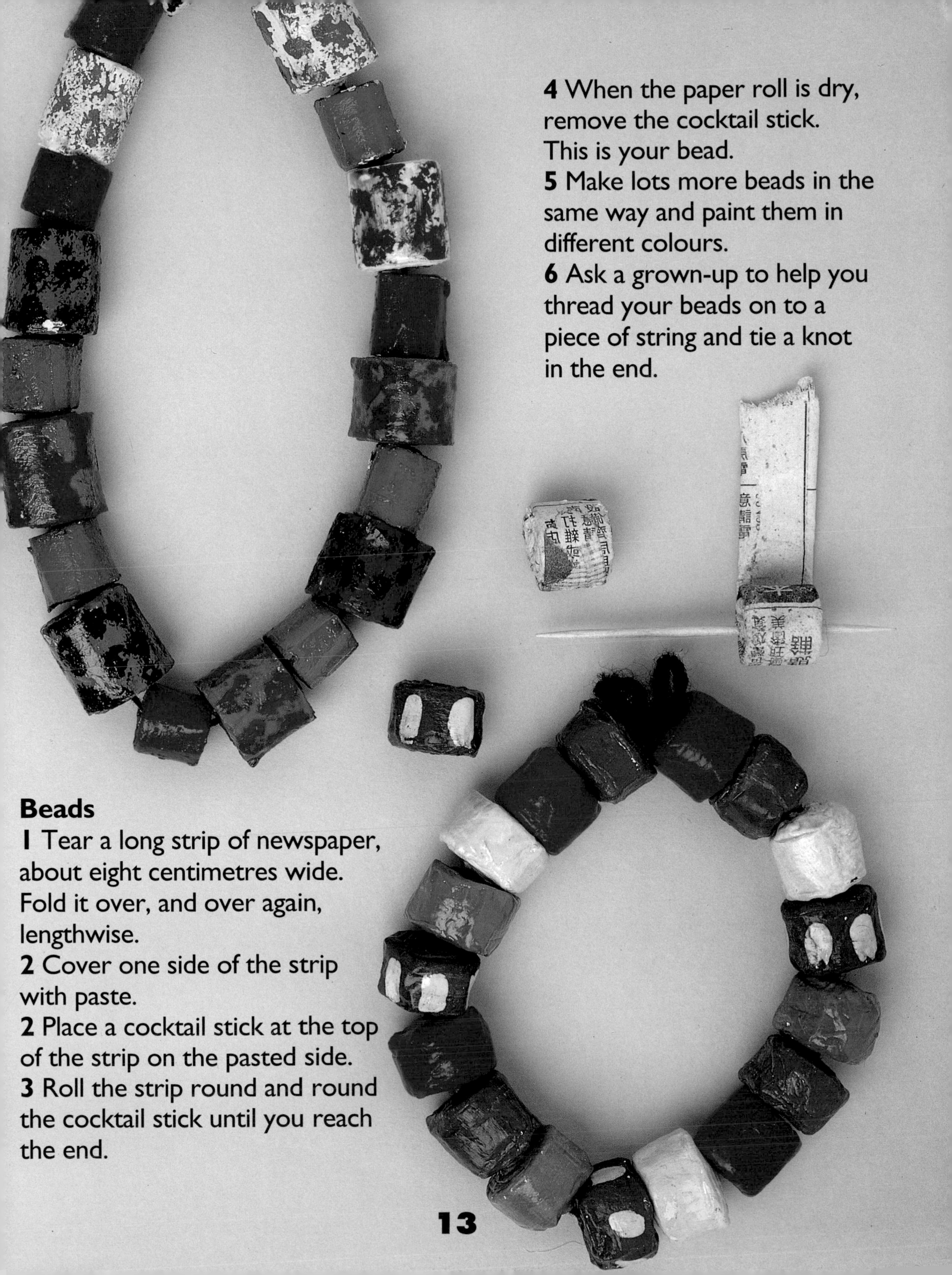

Beads

1 Tear a long strip of newspaper, about eight centimetres wide. Fold it over, and over again, lengthwise.
2 Cover one side of the strip with paste.
2 Place a cocktail stick at the top of the strip on the pasted side.
3 Roll the strip round and round the cocktail stick until you reach the end.
4 When the paper roll is dry, remove the cocktail stick. This is your bead.
5 Make lots more beads in the same way and paint them in different colours.
6 Ask a grown-up to help you thread your beads on to a piece of string and tie a knot in the end.

Bowls

Papier-mâché bowls can be used to hold all sorts of different things, and they are fun to make!

Ready, steady, go…

1 Blow up a balloon and knot the end.

2 Starting at the end away from the knot, cover about half of the balloon with layers of paper and paste. Leave it to dry.

3 To make a base for your bowl, cut a strip of thin cardboard. Curl it into a ring and tape the ends. It should easily fit the base of the balloon.

4 Cover the ring with strips of newspaper and paste. Let it dry.

5 Now, tape the ring to the base of the balloon. Use strips of paper and paste to cover the tape and make the join stronger.

6 Pop the balloon and take it out.

7 Ask a grown-up to help you trim the edge of the bowl.

8 Paint your bowl in bright colours.

Animals

Papier-mâché animals are easy to make. Look at the pictures here to find out how we made a spotty cow. With a bit of practice, you could make your own zoo, full of amazing animals!

Ready, steady, go...

1 To make the body, scrunch a sheet of newspaper into a fat, tube shape. Try and make it slightly pointed at one end for the head.
2 Wind some tape around the newspaper to hold it all in place.

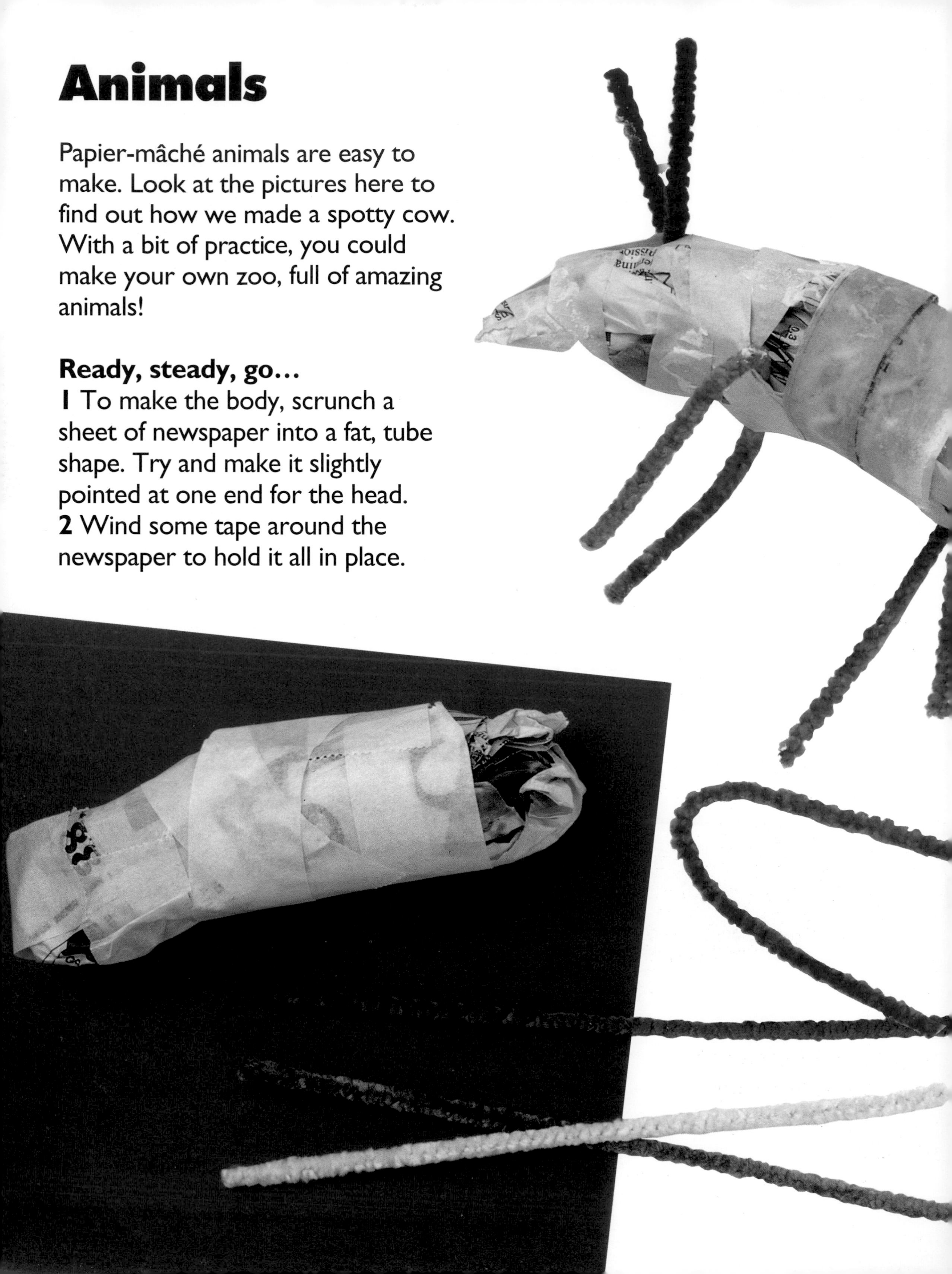

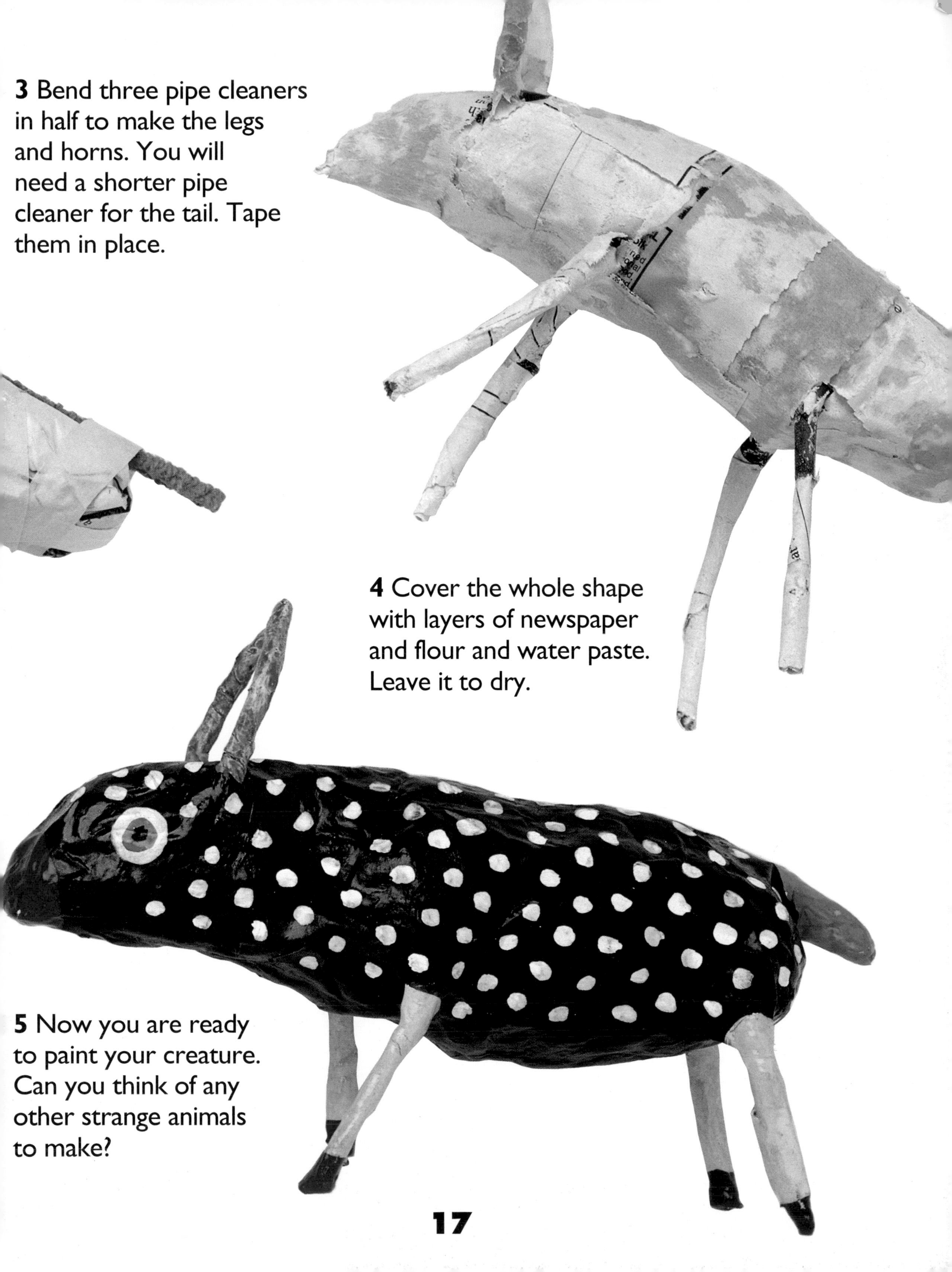

3 Bend three pipe cleaners in half to make the legs and horns. You will need a shorter pipe cleaner for the tail. Tape them in place.

4 Cover the whole shape with layers of newspaper and flour and water paste. Leave it to dry.

5 Now you are ready to paint your creature. Can you think of any other strange animals to make?

We made a tortoise and a bird to keep the spotty cow company!

The tortoise's shell was made using a balloon mould. The head, legs and tail were made from scrunched-up newspaper. The body and head of the bird were made from cardboard tubes. We made a paper cone for the beak.

Once you have made your basic animal shapes, you can cover them with paste and paper in the usual way.

Masks

We used a balloon as a mould to make these jolly masks.

Ready, steady, go…
1 Blow up a balloon.
2 Tear some newspaper into strips and make some paste.
3 Cover half of the balloon, lengthwise, with paper and paste.
4 When the paper is dry, pop the balloon and take the papier-mâché shape off.

5 Ask a grown-up to help you trim the edge of the mask and cut out two holes for your eyes.
6 You could hang your mask on the wall. But if you want to wear it, make two small holes, one on each side of the mask, at the same level as the eye holes. Thread lengths of string through to tie around your head.
7 To make a long nose, cut several strips of thin cardboard and tape them together. Then, tape the nose in position and cover it with paste and strips of newspaper.

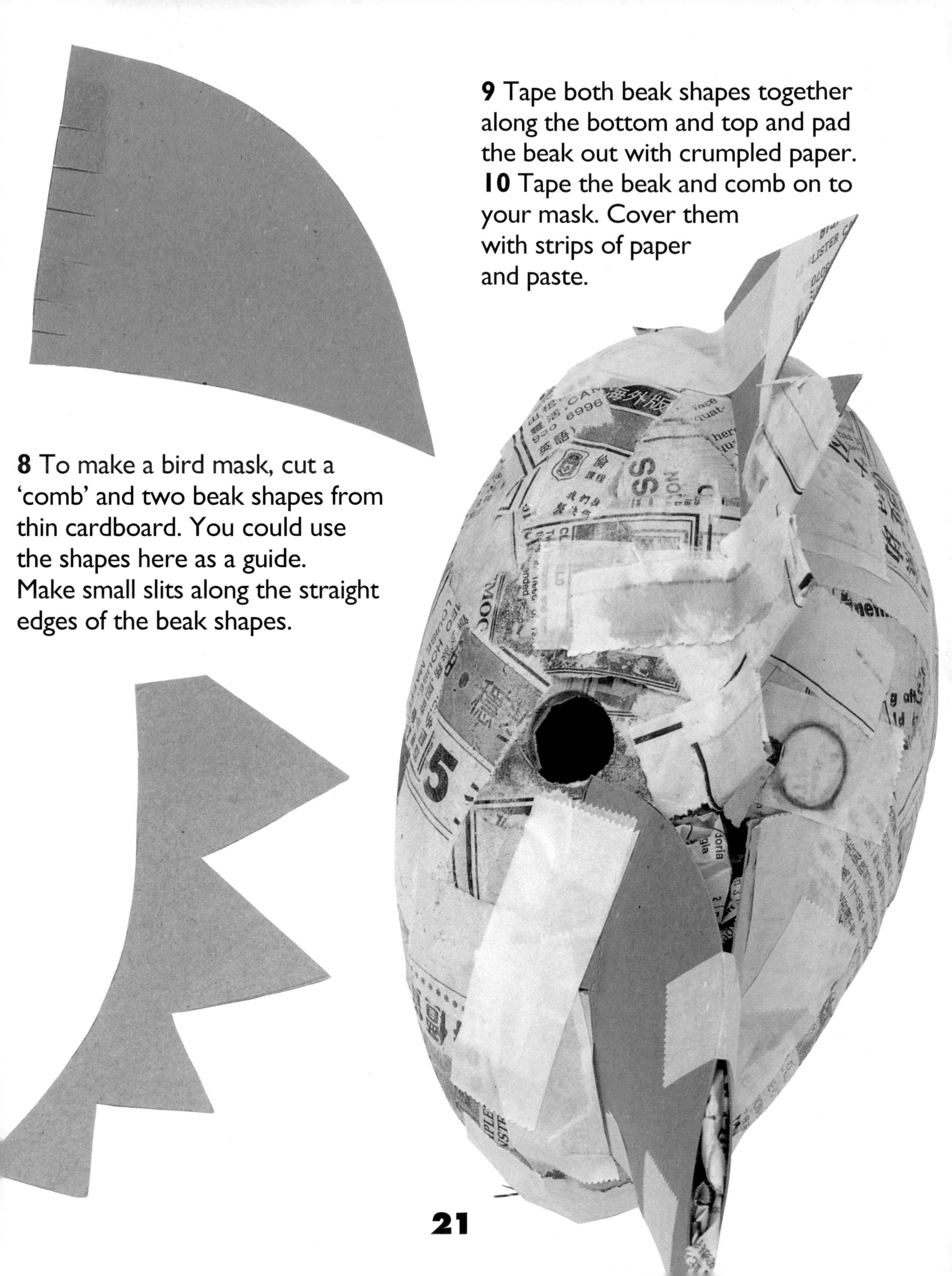

9 Tape both beak shapes together along the bottom and top and pad the beak out with crumpled paper.
10 Tape the beak and comb on to your mask. Cover them with strips of paper and paste.

8 To make a bird mask, cut a 'comb' and two beak shapes from thin cardboard. You could use the shapes here as a guide. Make small slits along the straight edges of the beak shapes.

When your mask is completely dry it is ready to decorate. You can draw a design on the mask first with a pencil, or coloured crayon. Then paint it in bright colours!

Why not make a collection of masks to decorate your bedroom wall? Or, for your next party you could invite all your friends to come wearing masks.

Index

animals 8, 11, 16, 17, 18, 19, 21, 23
badges 10, 11
balloons 3, 14, 18, 20
bangles 12
beads 13
bowls 14, 15
coloured paper 4, 5, 6,
masks 20, 21, 22, 23
moulds 2, 3, 18, 20
napkin rings 8, 9
paint 6, 9, 10, 12, 13, 14, 17, 22
paper plates 4, 5
picture frames 6, 7
pipe cleaners 16, 17
string 13, 20

If you have enjoyed this book look out for the full range

PLAY & DISCOVER ◆ What We Eat ◆ Rain & Shine ◆ Growing Up ◆ What We Wear

CRAFT ◆ Paint ◆ Paper ◆ Dress Up ◆ Fun Food ◆ Models ◆ Papier-Mâché

ANIMALS ◆ Pets ◆ On Safari ◆ Underwater ◆ On the Farm ◆ Birds ◆ Animal Homes

First Published in Great Britain In 1994 by
Two-Can Publishing Ltd., 346 Old Street, London EC1V 9NQ
in association with Scholastic Publications Ltd.

Printed and bound in Hong Kong 2 4 6 8 10 9 7 5 3 1

A catalogue record for this book is available from the British Library

Pbk ISBN 1-85434-242-8
Hbk ISBN 1-85434-241-X

Photographs by Toby

THE FIRST CHRISTMAS

Make a 3~D Model Nativity Scene

HENDERSON
PUBLISHING PLC

Once upon a time in a place called Nazareth, lived a young girl. Her name was Mary. She was warm-hearted and had a kind smile for everyone. Whenever a neighbour needed a helping hand, Mary would do her best to help. The village children often played near her little door, for Mary loved all the children and was especially patient with them.
Everyone who knew Mary liked her.

It would soon be the day of Mary's wedding. Mary was to marry a young man called Joseph who worked in the village. Joseph was a carpenter, making furniture for the people of Nazareth. He was not a rich man but he worked hard.

He hoped one day to make a comfortable home for his new wife, Mary. Their wedding day drew nearer and Mary was working hard too. She was busy sewing her wedding dress and cleaning the small house, ready for the wedding guests.

Every day, Mary worked hard. Yet when the afternoon sun baked hotly on the flat roofs of Nazareth and most of the villagers dozed in the shade, Mary would cover her young face with her shawl to protect it from the strong sun, and step out into the hot, dusty streets. Every day she walked to the little temple near her home. Mary loved God and kept a special place for Him in her heart. After her work was done, Mary would kneel under the cool white domed roof, and say her prayers to God.

One day, while Mary prayed quietly, a sudden bright light appeared just above her head. She looked up towards the light wondering what it could be. There, looking down at her, she saw an angel. Mary covered her face with her hands because she was very frightened. Then, in a voice that was soft and low, the angel spoke to Mary.

"Do not be afraid, Mary," the voice told her. "I am the Angel of the Lord and I bring you great news."

Mary turned her face toward the angel bravely. The angel, whose name was Gabriel, said, "You, Mary, are dearly loved by God. You are a good and kind woman. God is pleased with you and has chosen you to be the mother of His son. The time will come when you will have a baby. You will call him Jesus. This child will be King of all kings. He will be the Son of God."

Mary was deeply happy to be chosen by God.
"I am God's servant," she replied to Gabriel. "I will do what He asks of me, gladly." When Gabriel left Mary, she stayed quietly in the temple, thinking about God's important message to her.

That same evening, Joseph, the young man who was Mary's fiance, had a strange dream. The angel Gabriel appeared, telling him about God's wonderful gift to Mary. Joseph was a good, honest man and he loved God too. He promised the angel messenger that he would look after Mary and the precious child when it was born. And so, just as they had planned, Mary and Joseph were married.

The name Jesus means "God is with us". Perhaps you could find out what your name means?

Winter came to the land of Israel. From his throne room in a distant palace, the Emperor of Rome, Caesar Augustus, was making new laws. The Emperor passed one new law saying that all people living in his great empire must be counted. Under this law, people must register in the town where they were born. Joseph had been born in Judea, a long, long way from his home at Nazareth, in Galilee. He must return to Judea, taking Mary with him, to be counted.

The news of the new law worried Joseph. It would take several days to reach Judea. Then Joseph took some of the money he had been saving. With it, he bought a strong donkey, for his wife Mary was soon to have her baby and she couldn't possibly walk the long roads to Judea. Instead, Mary would ride on the donkey's back, as Joseph walked beside her.

They travelled the rough country roads, over stony paths and through rock-strewn valleys. Joseph guided the little donkey carefully all the way, and Mary never complained although the trip was long and uncomfortable. She wore her thick linen cloak wrapped across her shoulders to keep out the cold night air. All the way to Bethlehem they walked. Even the humble donkey was brave. Not once did he stumble on the jagged stones, but picked his way carefully on firmer ground as he carried Mary and her precious, unborn baby.

Night was falling as Mary and Joseph arrived in the little town. The roads were bustling with travellers. Some came on mules, like Mary. Many walked on tired feet, like Joseph. Some, the rich merchants, rode camels.
All came to Bethlehem to be counted for the Emperor's new law.

Both Mary and Joseph were very tired after their long journey. Joseph saw his wife's weary face and knew she could travel no further.
"You must rest tonight," he comforted Mary. "I will find a room for us." Then he walked, first from one guest house to another, looking for a room for the night. Everywhere he went, he was told, "We have no room".

They walked on through the dark streets and came to an inn. Joseph asked again for a room but the inn-keeper shook his head. "No. We have nothing to offer you. You'll find no-where to stay tonight. The town is full of people who have come to register for the Emperor."

Joseph's face grew worried.
"But my wife is due to have her baby very soon. Is there no-where at all?" The inn-keeper's wife appeared at the door. She was a kind woman and saw how tired Mary was. "There is the stable, at the back of the house, where the animals sleep. It might not be too comfortable but at least you can rest there."

Mary smiled at the inn-keeper and his wife thankfully.
"The stable will be fine," she said, quietly.

Bethlehem is in a country called Israel. Sometimes Israel is known as The Holy Land. Many people go there to visit the place where Jesus was born.

With a lantern in his hand, the inn-keeper led the way to the stable. It was nothing more than a small shed with straw scattered over the hard earth floor.

Joseph helped Mary down from the donkey. He laid his thick cloak over a mound of straw for Mary's bed. In the shadows of the stable, the soft noises of the inn-keeper's animals, an ox, a cow and two sheep, welcomed the weary travellers to their humble shelter that night.

Mary laid down to rest on the simple bed of straw. Almost at once, her weary eyes closed and Mary slept.

Joseph did not rest but looked around him. He knew the baby would soon be born, and he would need a little bed too. Then, Joseph saw the ox's manger.

With a corner of his robe, Joseph dusted down the wooden manger. Next, he gathered handfuls of clean straw from a bundle which the inn-keeper had left at the stable door. Joseph arranged the straw inside the manger.
Now, the new baby would have a crib for a bed.

It was very late that night when the footsteps of the last travellers passed by, and the narrow streets of Bethlehem grew silent at last.

One by one the lamps in the houses were put out. Even the inn stood in darkness. Only a tiny, yellow light burned from the stable.
Nothing stirred in Bethlehem.

In the night sky above the town, the new star shone ever brighter.

Below, came the sound of a tiny baby's cry. Jesus, Mary's son, was born.

Mary craddled her child gently in her arms. She wrapped him warmly in strips of cloth torn from her shawl. Happily, Joseph showed Mary the crib he had made ready, and together they laid baby Jesus to sleep in the manger.

The flickering light of a lantern shone warmly in the stable as Mary lulled Jesus to sleep, humming softly.

A manger for a bed
A manger is a wooden feeding box or trough that holds hay for cows and oxen to eat. It was just the right size for a baby to sleep safely in.

Silent Night

Silent night, holy night
All is calm all is bright
Round yon virgin mother and child
Holy infant so tender and mild
Sleep in heavenly peace
Sleep in heavenly peace

Silent night, holy night
Shepherds quake at the sight
Glories stream from heaven afar,
Heavenly hosts sing alleluia
Christ the Saviour is born
Christ the Saviour is born

Silent night, holy night
Son of God, love's pure light
Radiant beams from thy holy face
With the dawn of redeeming grace
Jesus, Lord at thy birth
Jesus, Lord, at thy birth

Angels are heavenly spirits made by God. The Angel Gabriel was a very special angel because he was chosen by God to do important work. Sometimes he appeared to people with a message from God, just like the one he gave to Mary.

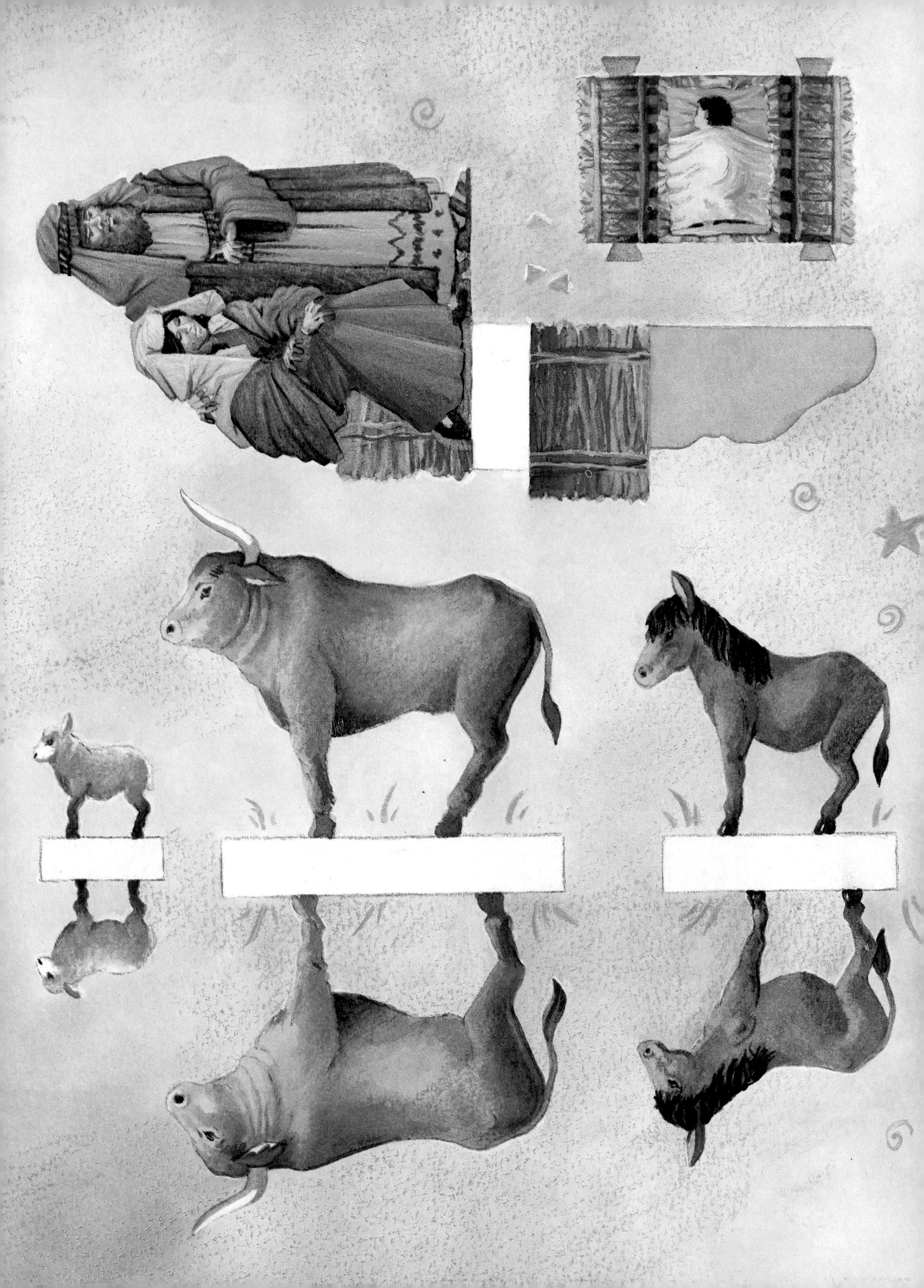

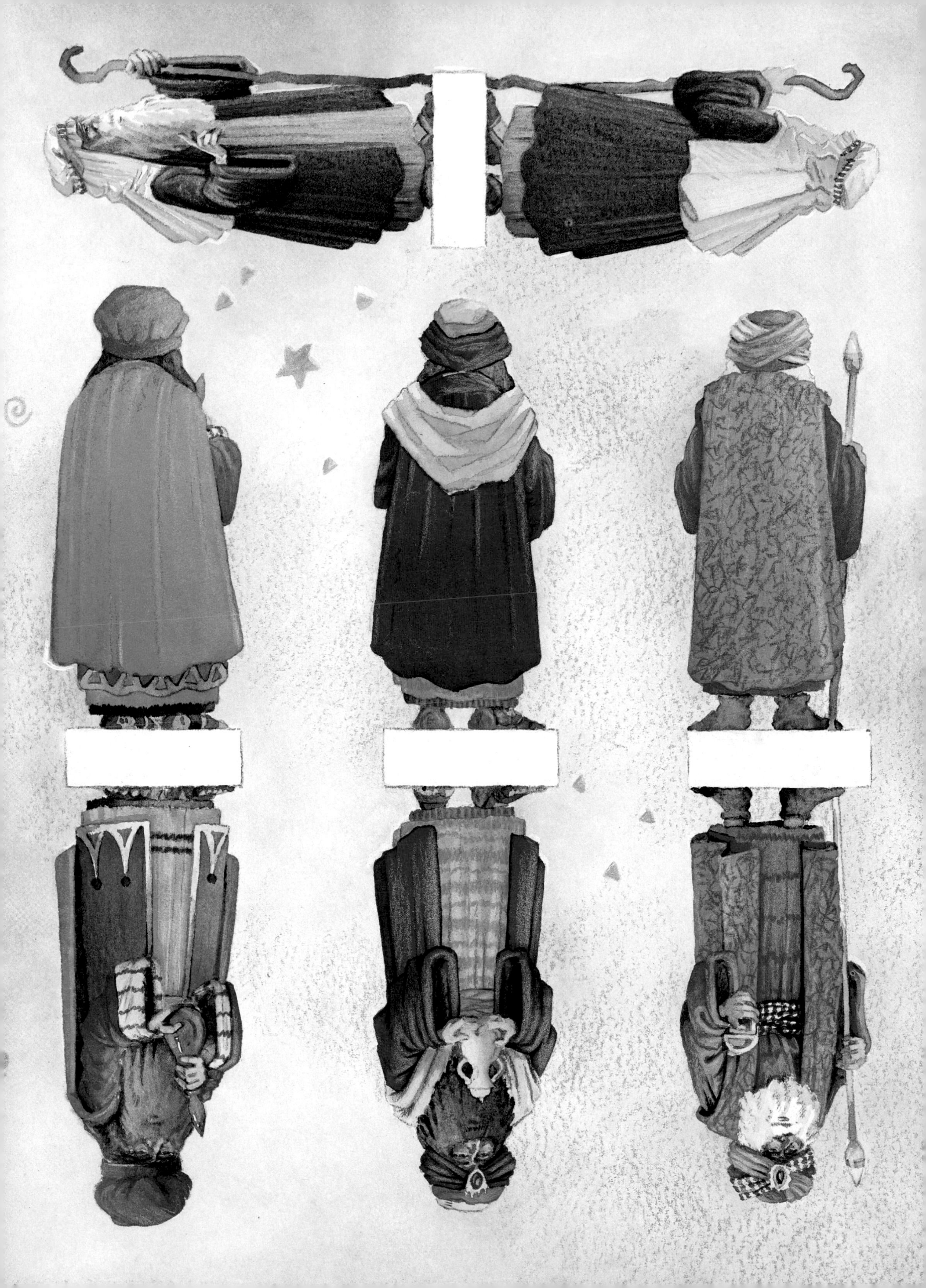

On a hillside just outside Bethlehem, a group of shepherds were watching their flocks of sheep as they grazed. The night had grown cold and the sheep settled down to sleep among the rocks. The shepherds covered themselves with heavy blankets and the three eldest huddled on the ground and began to sleep. The youngest shepherd was only a boy. It was his turn to keep watch over the animals. A sheep could stray from the flock and become lost, so the boy tried hard to stay awake.

Suddenly, a brilliant light lit up the sky above the hillside. The young shepherd boy gave a frightened cry which woke the men. Looking up, the shepherds saw a vision in a blaze of white light. An angel looked down on the men and spoke to them.

"Do not fear, for I bring you great news. Tonight, a child has been born. He is Christ the Lord. You will find him wrapped in simple cloth, and lying in a manger."

Then, to the wonder of the shepherds, a choir of angels appeared, singing and praising God. The night sky was filled with their heavenly voices.
"Glory to God in the Highest," they sang.

When the sky grew dark again, the excited shepherds made their plans.
"Let's go to Bethlehem and find this Lord the angel told us about."
"We will go and worship Him." They were all agreed. Quickly, they gathered up their belongings and set off on the long walk back to Bethlehem.

Carefully they found their way down the dark hill path. The shepherd boy picked up a small lamb and carried it gently in his arms.
"Here is my gift for the baby," he thought, happily.

The shepherds followed the bright star in the heavens, as the angel had told them to do. It shone its light over the tiny stable. The shepherds stepped quietly inside and Mary and Joseph welcomed the visitors kindly. Seeing where the baby Jesus lay, the shepherds knelt before the manger. Shyly, the little shepherd boy put down the lamb.
"For the baby King," he said.
Then the shepherds bowed their heads to pray.

Prayer
Jesus tender Shepherd, hear me!
Bless they little lamb tonight
Through the darkness be Thou near me
Keep me safe till morning light

O Little Town Of Bethlehem

O little town of Bethlehem
How still we see thee lie!
Above thy deep and dreamless sleep
The silent stars go by.
Yet in thy dark streets shineth
The everlasting light
The hopes and fears of all the years
Are met in thee tonight.

O morning stars, together
proclaim the holy birth
And praises sing to God the King
And peace to men on earth;
For Christ is born of Mary
And gathered all above
While mortals sleep, the angels keep
Their watch of wondering love.

How silently, how silently
The wondrous gift is given!
So God imparts to human hearts
The blessings of his heaven.
No ear may hear his coming,
But in this world of sin
Where meek souls will receive him,
Still the dear Christ enters in.

Many miles away from Bethlehem, in a far-off land, there stood a grand palace. It was the home of wise King Melchior. For years, this old king had studied the stars. He had learned that one day, a beautiful new star would appear in the sky. It would lead him to the birthplace of the King of all kings. King Melchior was overjoyed when, at last, the huge star hung in the sky.

He packed his bag, choosing a fine casket of gold for his gift to the young king.

He had been travelling for days when he met two more wise men. They were Caspar and Balthazar. They too were following the great star from the East. Like Melchior, they carried gifts for the new king, rare frankincense and myrrh.

The three kings travelled together on their camels for many more days following the bright star. At last, the star came to rest over a small town. It was Bethlehem.

The three wise men called at all the grand houses in the town, looking for the newborn king but they could not find him. Surely a king must be born in a palace, they puzzled together.

Then they came upon the stable, bathed in a halo of light from the star above it.
In surprise, they climbed down from their camels and entered the low stable. Mary held the young Jesus in her arms. When they saw the love shining from the young mother's face, their surprise left them. The wise men knew they had come to the right place after all. Here indeed, was the child who one day would be King of all kings.

Melchior stepped forward and spoke to Joseph.
"We have travelled across many lands to honour the boy who will be King." One by one, the wise men knelt in front of Mary and her child, laying their gifts on the bare stable floor.

GOLD was given as a sign of God's glory and majesty.
FRANKINCENSE, a sweet-smelling spice, was given as a sign that Jesus was the Son of God.
MYRRH, a rich spice with a bitter perfume, was given as a sad sign that Jesus would one day die on a cross.

We Three Kings Of Orient Are

Ve three Kings of Orient are,
Bearing gifts we traverse afar,
ield and fountain, moor and mountain,
Following yonder star.

HORUS:
O, star of wonder,
Star of night,
Star with royal beauty bright,
Westward leading, still proceeding,
Guide us to Thy perfect light.

elchior:
orn a King on Bethlehem plain,
Gold I bring, to crown Him again,
ing for ever, ceasing never,
Over us all to reign. CHORUS

Caspar:
Frankincense to offer have I;
Incense owns a Deity nigh:
Prayer and praising, all men raising,
Worship Him, God most high. CHORUS

Balthazar:
Myrrh is mine; its bitter perfume
Breathes a life of gathering gloom;
Sorrowing, sighing, bleeding, dying,
Sealed in the stone-cold tomb. CHORUS

Glorious now behold Him arise,
King, and God, and sacrifice!
Heaven sings alleluia,
Alleluia the earth replies. CHORUS

The First Noel

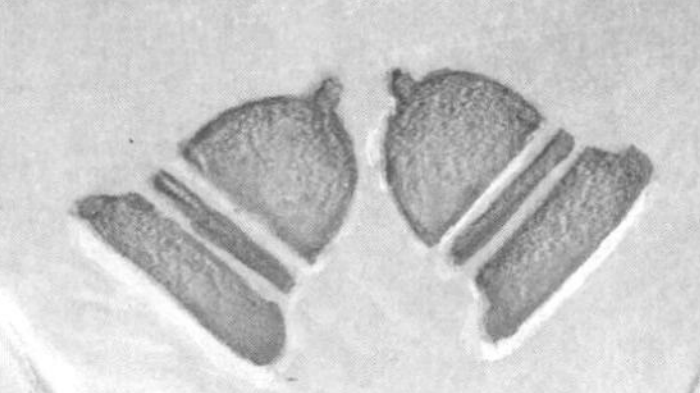

The first Nowell the angel did say
Was to certain poor shepherds in
fields as they lay;
In fields where they lay, keeping
their sheep,
On a cold winter's night that was
so deep:

Nowell, Nowell, Nowell, Nowell,
Born is the King of Israel.

They looked up and saw a star,
Shining in the east, beyond them far:
And to the earth it gave great light,
And so it continued both day
and night:

Nowell, Nowell, Nowell, Nowell,
Born is the King of Israel.

And by the light of that same star,
Three Wise Men came from
country far;
To seek for a king was their intent,
And to follow the star wheresoever
it went:

Nowell, Nowell, Nowell, Nowell,
Born is the King of Israel.

This star drew nigh to the north-west;
O'er Bethlehem it took its rest,
And there it did both stop and stay
Right over the place where Jesus lay:

Nowell, Nowell, Nowell, Nowell,
Born is the King of Israel.

Then entered in those Wise Men three,
Fell reverently upon their knee,
And offered there in his presence
Both gold and myrrh and frankincense:

Nowell, Nowell, Nowell, Nowell,
Born is the King of Israel.

Then let us all with one accord
Sing praises to our heavenly Lord,
That hath made heaven and earth
of naught,
And with his blood mankind
hath bought:

Nowell, Nowell, Nowell, Nowell,
Born is the King of Israel.

The meaning of Christmas

So, Christmas is a time when we celebrate the most famous birthday of all. Ever since that night long ago when Jesus was born in a stable, we honour him by decorating our homes and churches with holly, tinsel and pretty coloured fairy lights. We sing carols and give presents to each other, just as the shepherds and kings gave presents to Jesus. Christmas is a very special time of year for loving and giving.

At Christmas, play and make good cheer . . .
For Christmas comes but once a year!